LAKES
and
PONDS

Troll Associates

LAKES
and
PONDS

by Laurence Santrey

Illustrated by Holly Moylan

Troll Associates

Library of Congress Cataloging in Publication Data

Santrey, Laurence.
   Lakes and ponds.

   Summary: Describes the characteristics of lakes
and ponds, water-filled basins surrounded by land,
and explains how they are formed and how they can
be destroyed by pollution or human interference.
   1. Lakes—Juvenile literature.   2. Ponds—
Juvenile literature.   [1. Lakes.   2. Ponds.
3. Ecology]   I. Moylan, Holly, ill.   II. Title.
GB1603.8.S26   1984   551.48'2   84-2653
ISBN 0-8167-0206-3 (lib. bdg.)
ISBN 0-8167-0207-1 (pbk.)

High in the mountains, the crystal-clear water of a volcanic lake glistens in the sunlight. Far away, the wind blows across the dark blue surface of an ancient glacial lake. Out in the desert lies a strange lake with water that is saltier than sea water. And in another part of the country, a huge artificial lake holds drinking water that is used by people who live and work in a distant city.

Some lakes took millions of years to develop. Others suddenly appeared where no lake had been the day before. These are called sinkholes, because the ground caved in, or sank.

Some lakes have clean, cold water; and others are brown with mud and silt. Some grow larger in the rainy season and smaller in the dry season. And still other lakes never seem to change at all.

Many different kinds of lakes exist on every continent in the world—except the frozen wastes of Antarctica. But no matter where they are, how they were formed, or what kind of water they contain, all lakes have certain things in common.

Every lake is a body of water that fills a depression, or basin, in the ground. The water may enter from streams and rivers, bubble up from springs, fall from the sky as rain, or start as ground water that seeps up from deep in the soil.

A pond is another kind of water-filled basin that is surrounded by land. Ponds are very much like lakes, except for their size. A pond is usually much smaller than a lake. While a lake may be deep enough for large ships to use, a pond is much too shallow. In most ponds, green plants with roots can grow all the way from shore to shore. In lakes, these kinds of plants can grow only along the shallow shoreline.

Because a pond is so shallow, its water temperature is just about the same throughout. When the air temperature changes, the pond's water temperature changes with it. A lake, because it is much deeper, has different temperatures from top to bottom.

In summer, the surface of a lake may be quite warm, while the water near the bottom may be cold. And while the top layer of lake water may freeze in winter, the rest of the lake does not. A pond, however, is often shallow enough to freeze solid.

A large lake may have been formed in any of several different ways. These include the movement of ancient glaciers, shifting of the Earth's crust, volcanic activity, and the action of rivers.

Many years ago, the Earth's temperature was much colder than it is now. Huge sheets of ice, called glaciers, covered a large part of what is now North America and Europe. As the glaciers moved, they carried soil and rocks with them. This movement dug deep pockets in the ground in some places, and pushed up great piles of rock and soil in other places.

In time, the Earth warmed, and the ice melted. Water from the melting ice filled many of the pockets that had been gouged out by the glaciers, turning them into glacial lakes. Later, other land depressions were gradually filled up by rain and by melting snow that flowed down the mountainsides.

Four of the Great Lakes in North America —Lake Erie, Lake Huron, Lake Michigan, and Lake Ontario—were formed by glacial activity. The fifth Great Lake—Lake Superior—was formed by changes in the Earth's crust.

The Earth's crust, or thin surface layer, is made up of a number of sections called plates. From time to time, these plates shift, pushing against each other violently. Deep depressions or basins may be created on the surface of the Earth as the land shifts, shakes, and quakes.

These land shifts, or earthquakes, have created many lake basins besides Lake Superior. The world's deepest lake, Lake Baikal, in the Soviet Union, was created by a shifting of the Earth's crust.

Lake Baikal, which is more than a mile deep, is remarkable for other reasons, too. If all the fresh water in the world was divided into five equal parts, the water in Lake Baikal would be one of those parts. And living in this huge, deep lake are over 500 kinds of plants and over 1,000 kinds of water animals, most of which are found nowhere else on Earth.

Lakes also are created by volcanic activity. Crater Lake, in the state of Oregon, fills a depression that was left when a volcano collapsed thousands of years ago. No rivers or streams run in or out of Crater Lake. This lake's only sources of water are rain and snow.

A lake can also be formed when a river takes a new direction. Sediment simply piles up and closes off an old bend in the river. The old, closed-off portion is called an oxbow lake.

Still other lakes may be formed by beavers building a dam across a river or stream, or by people building a dam across a river valley. The lakes made by people are often used as reservoirs, to hold water for drinking or for irrigation. Often these artificial lakes are also used for recreation.

Ponds and lakes are home for many kinds of plants and animals. All of the plants and animals are closely linked in a life cycle called the food chain. Except for the energy supplied by the sun, everything the plants and animals need in order to survive is found in the food chain.

Microscopic, one-celled plants called algae are at the bottom of the food chain. They use the sun's energy to make food. Other green plants, such as the many-celled pondweeds, cattails, and grasses that grow along the shallow edges of a pond or lake, also use the sun's energy to make food.

The plants become the food for beetles, insects, and other tiny creatures that live in and around these waters. And these, in turn, are food for fish, turtles, snakes, frogs, salamanders, and other small animals.

At the top of the food chain in a pond or lake are large fish, raccoons, otters, minks, skunks, herons, egrets, and other such animals. These meat-eaters depend on the smaller creatures for food. There are also ducks, swans, and geese, beavers, musk-rats, and many kinds of rodents that are not meat-eaters. These animals eat the green plants that grow in or near the water.

The food chain that links all forms of life together keeps the pond or lake healthy and in balance. Even the dead plant and animal matter that falls to the bottom becomes part of the food chain. The minerals contained in this dead matter are used by the green plants.

If all the plants suddenly died, the food chain would be broken. The plant-eating creatures could not survive without plants to eat. The fish and birds that depend on the plant-eaters could not survive if their food source died. And then the larger creatures that hunt smaller ones could not survive either. Fortunately, the food chain is not often disturbed, except when people break it.

If people allow chemicals, pesticides, or sewage to be dumped into lakes and ponds, one or all of the links in the food chain can be broken, and the balance of nature will be upset.

If people build homes, factories, and roads too near a healthy pond or lake, the natural flow of water may be cut off. And as the pond or lake dries up, the plant life will die off.

If wastes from detergents and fertilizers are allowed to reach a healthy pond or lake, plant life may grow *too* fast. Then the pond or lake can be choked to death by its own vegetation.

Just a few years ago, many lakes and ponds all over the world were in danger of being destroyed because of pollution. Then efforts to clean them up and protect them were begun. The results have been very promising in many areas. For example, Lake Erie, once almost dead, now contains species of fish that could not live in it just a few years ago.

The Great Lakes and other lakes connected by rivers provide us with economical travel routes between the large industrial cities that have grown up along their shorelines.

We use many of our lakes for recreation—sailing, swimming, and fishing. In addition, lakes and ponds provide a practical source of water for irrigating crops of all kinds. Often, lakes and ponds help prevent floods and erosion by storing excess rainwater, instead of letting it rush across the land.

But even if they weren't so useful and practical, lakes and ponds would be popular for their natural beauty. For what could be more peaceful and lovely than a silent lake... with crystal-clear water...softly rippled by a gentle breeze?